GENESIS
A DOUBLE-EDGED
BIBLE STUDY

gen

—

GENESIS
A DOUBLE-EDGED
BIBLE STUDY

TH1NK **Life**Change

TH1NK, an
Imprint of
NavPress

NAVPRESS

Discipleship Inside Out®

NavPress is the publishing ministry of The Navigators, an international Christian organization and leader in personal spiritual development. NavPress is committed to helping people grow spiritually and enjoy lives of meaning and hope through personal and group resources that are biblically rooted, culturally relevant, and highly practical.

**For a free catalog go to www.NavPress.com
or call 1.800.366.7788 in the United States or 1.800.839.4769 in Canada.**

Cover design by Faceout Studio, Jeff Miller
Cover image by Shutterstock

Some of the anecdotal illustrations in this book are true to life and are included with the permission of the persons involved. All other illustrations are composites of real situations, and any resemblance to people living or dead is coincidental.

Printed in the United States of America

1 2 3 4 5 6 7 8 / 18 17 16 15 14 13

contents

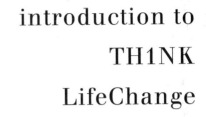

introduction to
TH1NK
LifeChange

Double-Edged and Ready for Action

For the word of God is alive and active. Sharper than any double-edged sword, it penetrates even to dividing soul and spirit, joints and marrow; it judges the thoughts and attitudes of the heart.

Hebrews 4:12

a reason to study

Studying the Bible is more than homework. It is more than reading a textbook. And it is more than an opportunity for a social gathering. As Hebrews suggests, the Bible knows us, challenges us, and yes, judges us. Like a double-edged sword, it's sharp enough to cut through our layers of insecurity and pretense to change our lives forever.

Deep down, isn't that what we want—to actually *experience* God's power in our lives, through Scripture? That's what TH1NK LifeChange is all about. The purpose of this Bible study is to connect you intimately with God's Word. It can change you, not only intellectually but also spiritually, emotionally, maybe even physically. God's Word is that powerful.

The psalmist wrote,

What you say goes, GOD,
and stays, as permanent as the heavens.
Your truth never goes out of fashion;
it's as up-to-date as the earth when the sun comes
up. . . .
If your revelation hadn't delighted me so,
I would have given up when the hard times came.
But I'll never forget the advice you gave me;
you saved my life with those wise words.
Save me! I'm all yours.
I look high and low for your words of wisdom.
The wicked lie in ambush to destroy me,
but I'm only concerned with your plans for me.
I see the limits to everything human,
but the horizons can't contain your commands!
(PSALM 119:89-90,92-96, MSG)

Do you notice the intimate connection the psalmist has with God *because* of the greatness of the Word? He trusts God, he loves Him, and his greatest desire is to obey Him. But the only way he knows how to do any of this is by knowing God's voice, God's words.

the details

Each TH1NK LifeChange study covers one book of the Bible so you can concentrate on its particular, essential details. Although every study exclusively covers a different book, there are common threads throughout the series. Each study will:

1. Help you understand the book you're studying so well that it affects your daily thinking
2. Teach valuable Bible study skills you can use on your own to go even deeper into God's Word
3. Provide a contextual understanding of the book, offering historical background, word definitions, and explanatory notes
4. Allow you to understand the message of the book as a whole
5. Demonstrate how God's Word can transform you into an authentic representative of Jesus

Every week, plan on spending thirty to forty-five minutes on your own to complete the study. Then get together with your group. Depending on the amount of time it takes, you can go through either a whole or half lesson each week. If you do one lesson per week, you'll finish the study in two and a half months. It's all up to you.

the structure

The ten lessons include the following elements:

Study. First you'll study the book by yourself. This is where you'll answer questions, learn cultural and biographical information, and ask God some questions of your own.

Live. After you've absorbed the information, you'll want to look in a mirror – figuratively, that is. Think about your life in the context of what you have learned. This is a time to be honest with yourself and with God about who you are and how you are living.

Connect. You know that a small-group study time isn't just for hanging out and drinking soda. A small group provides accountability and support. It's one thing to say to yourself, *I'm really going to work on this* and entirely another thing to say it to a group of friends. Your friends can support your decisions, encourage you to follow through, and pray for you regularly. And vice versa.

In your group, you'll want to talk with each other about what you've discovered on your own: things that went unanswered, things that challenged you, and things that changed you. Use the guidance in this section to lead your discussion. After that, pray for each other. This section will always provide targeted prayer topics for you and your group.

Go Deeper. Thirsty for more? Just can't get enough? Then use the guidance in this section to explore even more deeply the vastness of Scripture. It's similar to extra credit, for all you overachievers who love to learn.

Memory Verse of the Week. Did a particular verse make you think? Is there a verse you can't get out of your head? Write it down and memorize it. Allow God's Word to permanently brand itself in your head and your heart.

Notes. At the end of each chapter, there is space for notes. Use it to write notes from your group discussions, to ask questions of God or yourself, to write important verses and observations – or anything you want.

now go!

You are now ready to experience the Bible and the God of the Bible in an intense new way. So jump in headfirst. Allow the double-edged sword of Scripture to pierce your mind, your heart, your life.

Introduction to Genesis

beginnings

Have you ever started watching a show on TV in the middle of the series, and the characters all clearly have history with each other, but you have no idea what it is? Or have you tried reading the second book of a trilogy without having read the first one? Sometimes things make a lot more sense when you go back to the beginning and find out what happened.

That's a good reason to read Genesis. *Genesis* means "beginning," and the book of Genesis is all about beginnings. In it, God lays the groundwork for the rest of Scripture.

The Old Testament tells the story of how God worked through one nation to help the whole world. Genesis sets up that story by explaining how the whole world got into a mess in the first place. It then shows God choosing one family and promising to clean up the mess through them. Genesis traces that family through four generations – and they are not exactly Mr. and Mrs. Perfect and their little Perfects. They give God headaches, but He sticks with them, and by the end of Genesis the stage is set for the amazing things God will do in the book of Exodus. Genesis keeps reminding us that it's only the beginning of a story that will climax in the New Testament and not end until the vision of Revelation becomes reality.

Here's an outline to keep in mind as you read:

I. *Humans Mess Up (chapters 1–11)*
  A. *Creation*
  B. *The Fall*
  C. *The Flood*
  D. *The Tower of Babel*
II. *God Chooses a Family (chapters 12–50)*
  A. *Abraham*
  B. *Isaac*
  C. *Jacob*
  D. *Joseph and his brothers*

genesis and the new testament

Genesis is one of the top three Old Testament books quoted in the New Testament. The great themes of the New Testament all begin in Genesis. The garden of Genesis 2 with its river and tree of life returns in the garden-city at the end of Revelation. The serpent of Genesis 3 and the Babel/Babylon of Genesis 10–11 cause trouble throughout the Bible until they are finally defeated in Revelation. A series of prophecies in Genesis point toward Christ, who fixes what Adam broke.

If you've heard that the God of the Old Testament is mean and the God of the New Testament is nice, forget that. Just like in the New Testament, the God of Genesis has personal relationships with people, and He's committed to both justice and mercy.

rescue mission

Genesis doesn't tell us everything we might like to know about the history of the universe and humans because God never intended this book to answer those questions. Genesis focuses on God's plan to rescue humans from the results of their sin. The origin of the universe is relevant only in that it tells us some important things about who God is and what it was like to be human before sin corrupted us.

In the same way, when Genesis focuses in on one family, it's not because the people living in China and South America and Europe aren't important. It's because God is setting up that one family to rescue those other people all over the world from sin.

Genesis includes some lists of family lines that seem boring until you know why they're there. The book is organized into twelve parts with the repeated phrase, "These are the generations of _____":

- "These are the generations of the heavens and the earth" (Genesis 2:4, ESV) introduces the first generation of humans and what they did.
- "This is the book of the generations of Adam" (5:1, ESV) traces Adam's descendants to Noah.
- "These are the generations of Noah" (6:9, ESV) tells what happened in Noah's lifetime. And so on.

The story follows the trail of the chosen family after sketching the other branches of the family tree. For instance, we hear briefly about the descendants of two of Noah's sons but then more about the line of his third son, the ancestor of Abraham. The point is that through this one family line, all of the families in the world will eventually be blessed (12:2-3).

who wrote it and why?

Tradition attributes the first five books of the Bible to Moses. When the New Testament writers talk about the books of Moses, they are referring to Genesis through Deuteronomy. Moses shows up in the story in the book of Exodus.

Genesis was written for the chosen family, the nation of Israel. As you study it, try to imagine yourself as a member of that nation. Ask yourself questions like, "Who is this God we've committed ourselves to? What is our relationship to Him, and how did it come about? How did our people, Israel, come to be? What did God choose us to do, and why? How did God deal with the fact that we keep doing what we know we shouldn't do?" And, most importantly, "How should all this affect the way I live now?"

how it all started

Lesson 1

God created mankind in his own image, in the image of God he created them; male and female he created them.

Genesis 1:27

Where do you come from? Everybody has a story: where he grew up; parents or other caretakers who raised him; how that has or hasn't ruined him for life. Every nation also has a story: its Founding Fathers or royal line; the wars and other great events that have shaped it. And every culture has a story about how the world came to be and where human beings came from.

Did humans come about through the chance interactions of molecules? Is the physical world an illusion? Were we made – as the Babylonians believed – as an afterthought to feed and work for the gods? Is there anything unique about humans that makes us more than clever animals?

The first two stories in Genesis aren't intended to answer every question we have about human origins. They are meant to set the stage for the rest of the book by showing a few key things about God, humans, and the world humans live in. The first story (1:1–2:3) is a poem about God making the world, including us. The second (2:4-25) focuses in on God making the first man and woman.

If you haven't already read the introduction on page 13, do that now. It will give you the overview of what Genesis is about.

1 Read Genesis 1:1–2:3. As you read, write down words and phrases that are repeated. This is a prose poem, and it uses repetition the way song lyrics often do: to emphasize what's important, and to show where the natural divisions are.

2 Like seven verses in a song, the events of this poem are divided into seven days. Things start out "formless and empty" (1:2). Then on days one through three, God gives form to the formless darkness of chaos. In the left column of the following chart, write how God gives form to the formless.

On days four through six, God fills what was empty and puts something or someone in charge. In the right column of the chart, write how God does this.

Form		Fullness	
1		4	
2		5	
3		6	

On day 7, God rests to enjoy His work.

3 Write down what God wants us to learn about Him and the world from these repeated phrases:

"God said, 'Let . . . .' And it was so."

"It was good" and "It was very good."

4 What can we learn about humans from this story? What's important in 1:27-31?

> **fyi** **Image of God (1:27).** There are different views of what this may mean: (1) humans are like God in being able to reason and make moral choices; (2) humans are not just physical beings but are also spirit; (3) humans are capable of a spiritual relationship with God in ways animals are not; (4) God delegated His governing authority to humans on earth, so we were supposed to represent His good government over our planet.

5a Now read 2:4-25. What can we learn here about God's original intent for humans?

5b What can we learn about human nature and character (verses 7,25)?

5c What can we learn about the purpose and task God gave humans (verses 15,19-20)?

Helper (2:18,20). The Bible uses this word to describe God (see Hosea 13:9; Psalm 115:9-11) and military allies (see "staff" in Ezekiel 12:14), so "helper" does not imply inferiority. The sense is more of a needed ally than a servant girl.

fyi

6 What do 1:27-28 and 2:20-23 say to you about how women and men were meant to relate to each other?

7 What can we learn about God from the way He provided humans with a garden, a mighty river, many trees for food, and help/companionship in their work?

live

8   Think about the jobs God gave to the first humans: to govern the other animals (1:28); to work in and take care of the garden God made (2:15). What do you think doing these jobs *well* would involve? How well have humans done?

9   Lots of people today believe that humans are just animals with big brains that became the way they are by chance, and that there is no God who either made us or gave us a particular job to do. How do these beliefs affect a person's approach to life? (For instance, are people who think this way necessarily more selfish or aimless? Explain.)

10   Take a minute to praise God for something you saw in Genesis 1–2.

11   Ask God how He wants your life to be different after this study. Write down what you think He's saying.

connect

The opening chapters of Genesis offer an amazing number of things to fight about: How long did Creation take? Was evolution involved? And what about that whole girls-as-suitable-helper thing?

In your group, try very hard not to have these fights. Save evolution for another day. Skip the guy/girl competition. Instead, try to tune into what God wants you to get out of these chapters. What difference does it make that the physical world is good – not an illusion, not an evil snare, not a total and complete mess we need to escape as soon as possible – but good? What sort of God are we dealing with here? Why did God make us? Why does every human being have value, no matter what? And so what? How does all this affect you?

Spend some time thanking God for sharing the beginning of His story with us and ask Him to reveal new things to each member of your group over the course of this study.

go deeper

Compare gardens: Eden (Genesis 2), Gethsemane (Matthew 26:36-46), and the garden of Revelation 22:1-5. Compare the creation of the world in Genesis 1-2 to the future re-creation in Revelation 21–22. What similarities and differences do you see? Why do you think God isn't going to just put everything back the way it was before? What does that say about Him and His plan?

memory verse of the week

Did a particular verse make you think? Is there a verse you can't get out of your head? Write it down and memorize it. Allow God's Word to permanently brand itself in your head and your heart.

notes from group discussion

Lesson 2

The LORD God said to the
serpent . . . "I will put enmity
between you and the woman,
and between your offspring and
hers; he will crush your head,
and you will strike his heel."
Genesis 3:14-15

We've all done it. Even if there's only one thing we're not allowed to do, we do it. Somehow that one thing looks so good, it will feel so good, and it starts to be all we can think about. We make excuses. "It's not that bad." "God/my parent/my teacher is really mean to tell me I can't do that." "I'll do it just once, or just a little."

And then, when we do it, we blame somebody else. "So-and-so talked me into it." We're ashamed, but it's so hard to come clean.

This has been happening since the very first generation of humans. In Genesis 3–5 we'll see the pattern play out several times, and we'll see the consequences. We'll also see God taking action right from the start to save humans from themselves.

The tree of the knowledge of good and evil (2:9,17). It
isn't clear what this tree was, but the command in 2:16-17 was
apparently the only thing God told Adam not to do. There are two
ways to know good and evil: (1) You can know them by experience,
by doing them and experiencing the consequences, or (2) you can
know them by being taught and by observing what others do. For
instance, you can learn about drug addiction by using drugs (that's
the hard way), or you can learn about it without putting yourself
through that. God asked Adam to trust Him about when and how he
learned the difference between good and evil. He didn't want Adam
to learn by experience.

fyi

1a Read Genesis 3:1-24. There were lots of trees in the garden with
fruit that looked and tasted good (2:9). How did the serpent talk Eve
into eating the one fruit she wasn't supposed to eat (3:1-5)?

1b How might a modern person be tempted in a similar way?

I was afraid because I was naked; so I hid (3:10). Before
they did what they knew they shouldn't, Adam and Eve weren't
worried about being seen naked. They felt no shame (2:25). Shame is
a feeling we have when we fear that being exposed will harm us. We
feel shame about having our bodies or souls seen and then rejected,
mocked, punished, physically harmed, or just known to be inadequate.

fyi

2a After Adam and Eve ate the fruit, they felt shame. What were the things they did to avoid being exposed (3:7-13)?

2b What should they have done instead?

3 What are some things people do today to avoid being exposed when they have done something wrong?

fyi *Cursed (3:14,17).* Because of Adam and Eve's bad decision, the whole world changed for them and their descendants. Work that had been a creative pleasure became toil (3:17-19). Childbearing became painful and dangerous for women (3:16). But God made a promise: There would be conflict between the children of Eve and the children of the serpent, and one day a descendant of Eve would crush the serpent (3:15). Unfortunately, the children of Eve got off to a bad start.

4 Read Genesis 4:1-16. Adam and Eve's firstborn son was Cain. How would you tell this story from Cain's point of view?

5   God knew Cain's heart, so He was not impressed with Cain's worship. How would you tell this story from God's point of view?

6a   God responded to sin with *consequences* and with *love*. What consequences did He give in 3:9-24?

6b   In 4:10-16?

7a   Where do you see God treating wrongdoers with love in 3:9-24?

7b   In 4:10-16?

live

8   Can you identify with Adam, Eve, or Cain in any ways? If so, how?

9   Sometimes our lives are difficult because of what happened to the world after Adam and Eve sinned: Work is toil, and getting enough money to live on can be hard; marriage relationships are flawed; everybody is hiding and blaming other people for their problems. Write down at least one way the messed-up world affects you.

10   Sometimes we make our own lives more difficult: We hide; we blame others; we envy those who seem to be treated better than we are; we take out our anger on our brothers and sisters. Write down one way you make your life harder.

11   Given all this, how do you see God? Be honest. Does He seem like a harsh parent? Like a parent who is too busy to notice what you're going through? Does He care about your problems? Do you let Him close or push Him away or hide?

connect

Divide into two groups. Give one group some time to plan how to tell about Adam, Eve, the serpent, Abel, and God from Cain's point of view. How would Cain tell his family's story? Have one person write down what the group comes up with. Meanwhile, let the second group plan how to tell the same story from God's point of view. Is God mad, sad, emotionally detached? When you're ready, a spokesperson from each group can tell the story you came up with.

How are the stories alike and different? Which one is more accurate? How does this story affect the way you see God? The way you see yourselves? Spend some time thanking God for the character traits He has revealed about Himself through these chapters.

go deeper

A *type* is an Old Testament person, thing, or event that points forward to something in the New Testament. The term comes from the Greek word for a stamp that presses an image into something, like a bronze seal pressed into hot wax. Adam is a *type* of Christ, as the apostle Paul says, "Adam, who is a pattern [*type*] of the one to come" (Romans 5:14). Just as Adam was the first in a lineage of people who inherited the consequences of his sin, so Christ is the first in a lineage of people who inherit the consequences of His perfect life and sacrificial death. If we avoid pushing the similarities of a type and antitype too far, we can learn a lot from types. You can study the connections between Adam and Christ in Romans 5:12-19 and 1 Corinthians 15:20-22, 45-49.

memory verse of the week

Did a particular verse make you think? Is there a verse you can't get out of your head? Write it down and memorize it. Allow God's Word to permanently brand itself in your head and your heart.

notes from group discussion

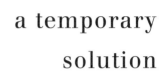

a temporary
solution

Lesson 3

Never again will I curse the ground because of humans, even though every inclination of the human heart is evil from childhood.

Genesis 8:21

You may have learned about Noah and his ark when you were little. Such a cute story: a ship full of animals! And they were all calm, and good-smelling, and docile, right?

The little-kid version of the story takes out the scary parts. After Cain, humans became more and more violent – so corrupt that God decided to drown them all and start over with Noah's family. And so Noah was instructed to complete an immense task: build the ark, a vessel that didn't make sense to the people of Noah's world. The ark was the size of a cruise ship, but the flood was no vacation. It was 270 days of bare survival.

study

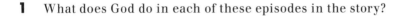

Righteous . . . blameless (6:9). Neither of these words means
sinless. *Righteous* means that Noah's relationship with God
was good because he trusted God and showed that trust by acting
with justice and obedience. *Blameless* means that Noah's neighbors
found no fault with the way he treated them.

1   What does God do in each of these episodes in the story?

Genesis 6:5-8

6:9-22

7:20–8:1

8:15-22

2   What impression do you get of God from each of these episodes?
How would you describe Him? Do you like Him? Why or why not?

Genesis 6:5-8

6:9-22

7:20–8:1

8:15-22

fyi *Covenant (6:18; 9:9).* A treaty or pact. In the ancient Middle East, there were covenants between equals, but kings also made covenants with their subjects.

3 Read Genesis 9:1-11. What were the terms of the covenant between God and His subjects (Noah, the animals, and their descendants)?

4a Where do you see God's justice in this story? (Or do you not see it?)

4b Where do you see God's mercy? (Or do you not see it?)

4c Does the Flood seem to you like a reasonable response to human wrongdoing? Why or why not?

live

5 Lots of people think of God as someone they can go to for help when life is hard, but otherwise He doesn't much matter. How does this idea of God compare to the picture of God in the story of the Flood?

6 Some people ask, "If God is perfectly good and all-powerful, why doesn't He solve the problem of evil in the world?" This story shows God tackling the problem of evil with a demonstration of sheer power. God has the power to kill all the evil people. He does it. But it doesn't solve the problem. Why not? And why is this helpful for us to know?

7   Some people think the God of the Bible is so horrible that they don't want anything to do with a God like that. How would you talk to such a person about God as He is portrayed in this story?

The Flood story isn't the whole story of God. It's an episode that points forward. So far in Genesis we've seen humans plunge into evil, and God has addressed the problem: (1) on a one-to-one basis with Adam, Eve, and Cain, and (2) on a worldwide basis with an act of raw power. He knows neither solution is permanent. He's setting up a solution that will take a lot longer but that will truly solve the problem. What will that solution be? Stay tuned.

connect

As a group, talk about the impression of God you get from this story. Is this someone you want to pray to, rely on, and obey? Why? Tackle one or more of the questions in the "Live" section with a rousing debate. Feel free to bring in the later episodes of the Bible's story (especially the part about Jesus sacrificing Himself), but don't lose sight of the Flood story, and don't think of the God of Noah as different from the God of the New Testament. How is the Flood story connected to what Jesus eventually does?

After you talk with each other, talk with God. What do you want to say to the God who drowned the evil people and then started over with a long, slow plan that would be painful to Him personally?

Read 1 Peter 3:18-22 and Romans 6:3-4. How is Noah's experience a *type* of Christian baptism? That is, how does it point forward to baptism?

Did a particular verse make you think? Is there a verse you can't get out of your head? Write it down and memorize it. Allow God's Word to permanently brand itself in your head and your heart.

notes from group discussion

a deeper problem

They said, "Come, let us build ourselves a city, with a tower that reaches to the heavens, so that we may make a name for ourselves."

Genesis 11:4

Why is cleaning even one bedroom a frustrating experience? Maybe because you've let the mess build up for too long, but *also* because it never stays clean for long. You knock yourself out, the place is spotless, and within days (if not hours) it's as bad as it ever was!

That's probably how God felt after the Flood. He cleaned out the muck of humanity, and the mud was hardly dry before one of Noah's sons was behaving like a runny-nosed loser. And things got worse: corruption and violence generation after generation. Fortunately, God wasn't surprised.

1   Read Genesis 9:18-28. Here we have Noah, who was righteous and blameless back in 6:9. And we have his son Ham. What's wrong with what Ham does? What does his action say about his character?

Genesis 10 portrays the peoples of the Middle East, Africa, and the Mediterranean as descendants of Noah's three sons. The point of these genealogies is that Genesis is about to focus down on a single family, but God still has in view a plan for all the nations of the world.

Tower that reaches to the heavens (11:4). Many temple-towers were built in Mesopotamia (modern Iraq and parts of neighboring countries) between 2800 and 2200 BC. The Babylonians developed the zodiac and horoscope so they could learn and control human destiny by reading the stars. These towers were used for astrological readings and for rites to connect the earth with the heavens.

fyi

2   Read 11:1-9. Compare 11:1-2 to 11:9. What has changed?

3   The first "Come, let's . . ." is said by the humans (11:3). Write down what's wrong with their goal . . .

to make a name for themselves

to reach the heavens and contact the gods of the stars so as to control nature and human events

fyi **Come, let us (11:3,4,7).** The story in 11:1-9 is built with a literary structure called a *chiasm*: ABCBA. This structure (like an X) was considered elegant in the ancient world, and lots of stories in the Bible use it.

11:1-2	narrative
11:3-4	spoken lines: "Come, let's . . ."
11:5	turning point
11:6-7	spoken lines: "Come, let us . . ."
11:8-9	narrative

The "Come, let us" in 11:6-7 is an ironic twist on the one in 11:3-4.

4a How do people today go about trying to make a name for themselves?

4b How do people today try to control nature and human events?

4c Is it possible to go after these goals and still treat God as God? If so, how? If not, why not?

5 Verse 6 explains why God frustrated these people's attempt to unite and accomplish their goal. What are the dangers of humans uniting their power if they haven't dealt with their deep-rooted selfishness and corruption?

6 By scattering the peoples and confusing their languages, God kept them from forming one united empire to pursue evil goals. But this was another temporary solution. From what you know of world history up to the present day, why couldn't this be a permanent solution to the problem of human evil?

live

7   Have you ever done something to make a name for yourself? Maybe at your school or online? If so, why does/did making a name for yourself matter to you? How has it worked out so far? If not, what keeps you from doing that?

8   What would you like to say to God in response to what you've been studying?

connect

Read aloud 11:1-9 like a play. Have different group members read the roles of narrator, the people who want to build the Tower, and God.

As a group, talk about ways you've tried to make a name for yourselves. Why are fame and popularity so important to so many people today? What are the things about our culture that make fame seem so appealing? Where do you see celebrity culture in the church? How does that affect the church? How could you go about trying to make your life count for something good without being driven to be popular or famous – and without feeling ashamed if you're not popular or famous?

In your group or with a partner, take it to the Lord and confess any areas of your life that are more focused on your own fame than God's. Ask Him to strengthen and guide you as you seek to put Him first.

go deeper

On the day of Pentecost, God reversed the confusion of languages that He started at Babel. Read Acts 2:1-13. What did this event mean? Compare the unity in Christ that God planned for mankind (see Ephesians 2:11-22; 4:1-16; Revelation 5:6-10; 7:9-10) to the unity of Babel. How are the goals different? How is unity in Christ accomplished?

memory verse of the week

Did a particular verse make you think? Is there a verse you can't get out of your head? Write it down and memorize it. Allow God's Word to permanently brand itself in your head and your heart.

notes from group discussion

abraham and sarah

Lesson 5

I will make you into a great nation, and I will bless you; . . . and all peoples on earth will be blessed through you.

Genesis 12:2-3

When we hear about all the violence and cruelty in our world, sometimes we wonder how a good God could let it happen. If God is all-powerful, why did He let the Holocaust happen? Or the senseless deaths of children? Or the poverty and violence some of us have experienced?

There are no easy answers to the problem of evil. But part of the answer is that unless God destroys all humans or makes us robots without the freedom to make moral choices, getting rid of evil is a long, slow process. When Jesus became a man and died for us, He struck a decisive blow against evil. One day He will come again to deal the final blow. But until then, the work is ongoing.

One of the key moments in this process came when God began to shape a particular family into the nation in which Jesus would eventually be born. Genesis 12 tells us how God started a relationship with one couple – Abram and Sarai – who raised goats and sheep in Iraq. The fate of the world hinged on their choices, and on God's faithfulness despite their choices.

1 Read Genesis 12:1-3. God told Abram to do one thing: leave his familiar world and move to Canaan. What did God promise to do in return?

---

fyi

Harran . . . Canaan (12:5). Harran was a trading center on the Euphrates River in what is now Iraq. Canaan (modern Israel/Palestine) was about four hundred miles from Harran, and lots of people already lived there. Harran had a stable water supply from the river, but Canaan had only closely guarded wells and springs where foreigners like Abram had to pay for water. If rainfall was low, the springs dried up and there was famine.

Moving four hundred miles was much harder than it is now. People relied on their extended families to provide what we expect from police and government. If you and your spouse and your herds went hundreds of miles away, there was no one to protect you from criminals or help you in hard times. Travel back and forth took months through dangerous land. Think of moving to some remote and unstable part of the world with no telephone, Internet, ships, or airplanes.

2 The people of Babel tried to make a name for themselves (11:4). God told Abram, "I will make your name great" (12:2). And God did make Abram's name great – long, long after Abram was dead. Think about what God offered Abram in exchange for completely turning his life upside down. Would it be worth it to you? Why or why not?

3a Abram is famous in the New Testament for his faith in God. Read Genesis 12:10-20. How was Abram doing at faith in this early stage of his relationship with God? What did he do to show faith or the lack of it?

3b How did God fulfill His promise from 12:2-3 in this situation?

3c What do you learn about God from this episode?

fyi **Sleep with my slave (16:2).** This was a legal way to get an heir. It was a form of surrogate motherhood. Hagar's child would be counted as Sarai's.

4a Years passed. God had promised to make Abram into a great nation, but Abram and Sarai didn't have even one child. Genesis 15 tells us how God encouraged them to keep trusting Him. Then more years passed. Read Genesis 16:1-16. How did Sarai deal with the long wait for a child?

4b How did Abram respond?

4c What were the results of their choices?

Circumcision (17:11). This was the physical sign of the covenant between God and the descendants of Abraham. It was saying to God, "I am set apart for your service, cut apart from the world. And if I fail to be loyal in faith, surrender, and obedience to you, may you cut me off from my life and your presence as I have cut off the foreskin of my body."

fyi

5a Abram was 99 years old when God appeared to him yet again to reaffirm their covenant. Read Genesis 17:1-27. What promises did God make at this point?

5b What did God ask Abram/Abraham to do in response? How would Abraham live out his faith in God's promises (17:1,9-10)?

live

6 God told Abraham, "walk before me faithfully and be blameless" (17:1). What do you think it means to walk before God faithfully? (See also the note on "blameless" in lesson 3, page 35.)

7a One of the challenges of studying stories in the Bible is that they tell us what people did, not necessarily what they should have done. We're often expected to tell the good from the bad based on what we're told about right and wrong elsewhere in the Bible. What were some of the things Abraham and Sarah did wrong?

7b God didn't reject them because of their bad choices, but those choices still had consequences–for them and even more for other people. Suppose Abraham and Sarah said, "Nobody's perfect. We made mistakes. But God counts Abraham's faith as righteousness (15:6), and that's good enough." What would Hagar and Ishmael say about that?

8 What would you like to say to God about Abraham and Sarah's story? Do you have questions you'd like to ask God? Do you identify with Abraham or Sarah (or Hagar or Ishmael) in any ways?

connect

Divide your group into four subgroups. Give yourselves some time to figure out how to tell the story of Abraham and Sarah from these different points of view:

> Subgroup 1: Abraham
>
> Subgroup 2: Sarah
>
> Subgroup 3: Hagar
>
> Subgroup 4: God

Then bring the subgroups back together and let one volunteer from each group tell or read the story from that point of view. What do you learn from the differences? How does God take into account Abraham's faith and his bad choices, God's forgiveness of Sarah and the needs of Hagar, God's long-range plan for the world and the short-range issues of these people?

Focus your group prayer time on what you've learned about God's forgiveness and His plan for your lives. Thank Him for the examples of His faithfulness in the lives of Abraham, Sarah, and Hagar.

go deeper

In Romans 4, the apostle Paul draws some conclusions from the story of Abraham and applies them to our lives. What does Paul say about Abraham's faith? About God's promise? About the command to circumcise Abraham's descendants? How is all this relevant to us?

memory verse of the week

Did a particular verse make you think? Is there a verse you can't get out of your head? Write it down and memorize it. Allow God's Word to permanently brand itself in your head and your heart.

notes from group discussion

a visit from God

Lesson 6

Will not the Judge of all the earth do right?

Genesis 18:25

There are good neighborhoods to live in, and there are not-so-good neighborhoods. It's not about how much money the neighbors make or what their ethnic background is. It's about how they live. Do they prowl in violent gangs, break into people's homes, and assault strangers? That's not a good neighborhood.

When Abraham moved to Canaan, he brought with him his nephew Lot. Lot thought he was a smart guy. He had herds of sheep and goats as Abraham did, and the two men split up so that their herds wouldn't compete for grazing land. But Lot settled in a bad neighborhood. Not a poor neighborhood – a rich, bad one. Abraham did what he could to get his nephew out of trouble, but when you move in next door to trouble, trouble is going to happen to you.

study

fyi

Men (18:2). Two of them were angels (19:1). The third might have been God Himself (18:1,13,17,20,22,26,33). Abraham and Sarah were blessed to have been visited by these men, as they were given unexpected promises and were able to speak openly with them.

1a Read Genesis 18:1-15. Why do you think Sarah laughed when God promised she would have a son the following year?

1b Why did she lie about having laughed?

fyi

Sodom (13:12-13; 18:16). One of several walled cities in what is now the southwestern portion of the Dead Sea. These cities were wealthy and decadent (13:10,13). Ezekiel 16:49-50 tells us that the worst sin of Sodom was not sexual, it was that the people were "arrogant, overfed and unconcerned; they did not help the poor and needy."

2a Read Genesis 18:16-33. What does the Lord reveal to Abraham as He and the angels are leaving Abraham's tents?

2b When Abraham asks the Lord not to deal with Sodom the way He dealt with the whole world in Noah's day, what reason does Abraham give?

3a How would you describe Abraham's attitude toward the Lord when he goes on to bargain with Him? How respectful is he?

3b Do you think the Lord welcomes this bargaining or only tolerates it? Why?

3c Do you think this is meant to be an example of how we might pray for people? Or was Abraham a special case? Explain your thinking.

4a Read Genesis 19:1-29. What do you learn about the people of Sodom? What do they do? What character qualities do they show?

4b What do you learn about Lot? What does he do? What character qualities does he show?

4c What do you learn about God?

5 Read Genesis 19:30-38. How has their upbringing in Sodom and with a father like Lot (19:8) shaped their character?

6 Why do the angels save Lot's family? Do you think Lot deserves to be rescued from Sodom? What about his daughters?

live

7 Think about the people you spend time with. How have they influenced you in good and/or bad ways? Try to think of some specific situations and list them here.

8 How are you moved to pray in response to what you've studied? Is there anybody you'd like to pray for – someone else or yourself? Write your prayer in the space below.

connect

Read aloud Genesis 18:16-33 like a play. Have different people read the roles of the narrator, the Lord, and Abraham. If you like, you can read 19:1-29 as a play too, with the roles of narrator, angels, Lot, and the people of Sodom.

Discuss your reactions to the destruction of Sodom. Do you like to see God responding to wickedness with justice? Or does this kind of violence make you uncomfortable with God? Would you like God to deal with wickedness in this way today? Are you surprised that Ezekiel 16:49-50 says Sodom's worst problem was the people's pride and lack of concern for the poor?

In your group, pray for one another about any unease you may be feeling about God's character. Also ask Him to reveal and help you address any sin that may be holding you back from His good plans for your life.

go deeper

Genesis 14 tells how Abram rescued Lot when some Mesopotamian kings tried to conquer Sodom and nearby cities. Abram refused to accept thanks from the king of Sodom because he wanted no alliance with those cities, but he did accept an alliance with Melchizedek, the king of Salem (Jerusalem). Read the curious story of Melchizedek in Genesis 14, and then explore how the writer of Hebrews sees him as a type of Christ (see Hebrews 7).

memory verse of the week

Did a particular verse make you think? Is there a verse you can't get out of your head? Write it down and memorize it. Allow God's Word to permanently brand itself in your head and your heart.

notes from group discussion

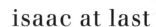

isaac at last

Lesson 7

Take your son, your only son,
whom you love – Isaac. . . .
Sacrifice him.

Genesis 22:2

Some people think of God as their best friend, the person who is always there when they need someone to listen and understand, the person who will fix things when things go wrong. And there's a lot of truth in this view. God is always there to listen and understand, and He does often fix things when we pray. But if that's where our understanding of God begins and ends, we're not dealing with the real God.

God made and kept huge promises to Abraham. He got Abraham out of trouble over and over. And He gave Abraham what he wanted more than anything else in the world: a son. But God also asked Abraham to follow Him into some incredibly hard places. God asked this because faith in God-my-personal-therapist-and-servant isn't enough. The only faith that counts is courageous faith in the real God.

Isaac (17:19; 21:3). God chooses Isaac's name, just as He chose Abraham's and Sarah's names. Isaac's name means "he laughs."

1a Read Genesis 21:1-7. Why do you think God chooses to name Isaac "he laughs"? Who is laughing? What is the joke? (See also 17:15-19; 18:9-15.)

1b What does this joke say about God?

Moriah (22:2). The Jewish temple was later built on Mount Moriah (see 2 Chronicles 3:1), and it became the only lawful place for sacrifice. Another hill in the region of Moriah was later called Golgotha (see Mark 15:22) or Calvary. Jesus was crucified there.

2 Read Genesis 22:1-2. What is God asking Abraham to give up by sacrificing Isaac?

3   Read Genesis 22:3-8. Abraham tells his servants, "we will come back to you" (22:5). He tells Isaac, "God himself will provide the lamb for the burnt offering" (22:8). What does Abraham believe about God? (You could look at Hebrews 11:19.)

4   Read Genesis 22:9-18. Abraham's willingness to sacrifice Isaac proves that he fears God (22:12). What does the angel mean by that phrase "fear God"?

5   What impression of God do you get from 22:1-18?

6   A similar event happens in the New Testament. In that event, Jesus takes the position of Isaac, and God the Father takes the position of Abraham (see John 3:16). What impression of God do you get when you put the two stories side by side?

live

7a God sometimes asks us to put into His hands the person or thing we value most, and to keep trusting and following Him even if He doesn't give that person or thing back to us. What are some examples of people or things God might ask someone to entrust to Him in this way?

7b Try to think of something specific in your own life that God might ask you to entrust to Him. Do you know for sure what your response would be?

8 How is fearing God different from seeing God as your best friend who is always there for you? How would fearing God affect what you do and don't do?

9 Do you fear God? Do you think you should fear God? Can you fear Him and trust Him at the same time, as Abraham did?

connect

Isaac is old enough to carry the wood for the fire (22:6). It takes a considerable amount of wood to burn an animal, so Isaac must be a preteen or teen. As a group, discuss what Isaac must believe about his father and God that keeps him from fighting for his life when Abraham ties him up and puts him on the altar (22:9). How does

70

Isaac relate to God after this experience? Why does he later pass on faith in (and fear of) God to his own children instead of deciding he wants nothing to do with this God? Spend some time in prayer for one another to be strengthened in faith.

go deeper

God promised the whole land of Canaan to Abraham. Genesis 23 tells how much of the land Abraham owned by the time he died. Read Genesis 23:1–25:11. How much land did he own? What does it tell you about God that this promise wasn't fulfilled until hundreds of years later? How do you relate to a God who takes hundreds of years to fulfill His promises? Is that too long for you? Why or why not?

memory verse of the week

Did a particular verse make you think? Is there a verse you can't get out of your head? Write it down and memorize it. Allow God's Word to permanently brand itself in your head and your heart.

notes from group discussion

notes from group discussion

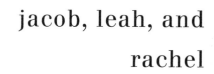

jacob, leah, and rachel

Lesson 8

Surely the LORD is in this place, and I was not aware of it.

Genesis 28:16

Nobody's perfect. In fact, most of us are hundreds of unpaved miles from perfect. Some of us try so hard to be perfect it makes us nuts – but some of us have, well, the opposite problem. Somehow, we got the idea that because perfection is impossible, growing up is optional. We want to hit that magic age of eighteen and stay there forever, doing whatever we want whenever we want to do it.

The Bible paints a very different picture of what God wants for us. God put Abraham through several decades of Marine-style training in faith, with a grueling final exam. Abraham had to choose whether or not he would entrust the life (and death) of his son, Isaac, into the hands of God. Isaac had to decide, in that terrifying moment, whether he was going to stretch out on an altar. And now God's promise to redeem the whole world through a single family is in the hands of Isaac, his wife, Rebekah, and their two sons, Jacob and Esau. As you'll see, Jacob is a manipulative jerk as a teen (you may recall Abraham telling one or two whopping lies, so it appears to run in the family). But God is going to put Jacob in a blender and turn it on high. He won't come out perfect, but he will come out a man.

Jacob (25:26). The name means "May he be at the heels." In other words, "May God have your back." But the name could also describe a person who dogs another's heels, takes the other's place, deceives, or betrays. In a positive sense it could describe someone who holds on to his goals and responsibilities.

fyi

1 Read Genesis 25:19-34. What do you learn about each of the characters in this story? What does each person do?

Isaac

Rebekah

Jacob

Esau

fyi *Birthright (25:31).* This includes the firstborn's right to a double portion of the inheritance as well as the leadership of the family after the father's death.

2   Read Genesis 27:1-40. How would you describe each of these characters now? What sort of people are they?

Isaac

Rebekah

Jacob

Esau

3   Read Genesis 27:41–30:23. Make a list of:

things that happen to Jacob

choices he makes

4 How would you describe Jacob's relationship with God based on 28:10-22? In what ways is God at work in his life? What does he understand about God? Is there anything he doesn't yet understand?

5 Do you feel sorry for Jacob when his uncle cheats him? Why or why not?

Disgrace (30:23). In that culture, women were valued mainly if they bore sons. Barrenness was seen as a failure, the inability to fulfill a woman's most valuable function.

6 Do you feel sadder for Leah or for Rachel? (Or for neither of them.) Why?

7   What do you make of the fact that God chooses people like this
to be the family who will carry forward His plan for a nation in
which the Savior will be born? Do they deserve it? Does that
matter?

live

8   What are some blessings you have that you did nothing to
deserve?

9   How do you feel about the idea of God putting you through hard
things in order to help you grow fully into the human being He
created you to be? Should He do that, or would you rather stick with
"Nobody's perfect"? Does the idea of God wanting you to become
mature fit with your idea of a God who loves you unconditionally?
Describe your thoughts and feelings below.

connect

Talk about God's promise to Jacob: "I am with you and will watch
over you wherever you go" (28:15). How does God watch over Jacob?
What are some things that happen to Jacob that would make him say,
"Yes, that's God watching over me"? What are some things that

happen to him that might make him wonder whether God is still there?

Then share your own experiences with each other. Do you ever wonder whether God is watching over you? What sorts of things make you wonder? What experiences have made you say, "Surely the LORD is in this place, and I was not aware of it" (28:16)? Pray for each other, either thanking God for the ways He is with each person, or asking Him to watch over them in the hard situations. Try to share specific requests with each other.

go deeper

According to the apostle Paul, what does the case of Jacob and Esau reveal about God (see Romans 9:10-16)? Does that seem unfair to you? Why or why not? Does it affect your view when you consider that the descendants of Esau (and the rest of us who aren't Jacob's descendants) eventually received God's grace through Jesus, a descendant of Jacob. In light of this fact, was God cruel to choose Jacob and reject Esau?

memory verse of the week

Did a particular verse make you think? Is there a verse you can't get out of your head? Write it down and memorize it. Allow God's Word to permanently brand itself in your head and your heart.

notes from group discussion

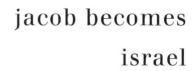

jacob becomes israel

Lesson 9

The man said, "Your name will no longer be Jacob, but Israel, because you have struggled with God and with humans and have overcome."

Genesis 32:28

It's infuriating to be manipulated. Some people seem so friendly and easygoing, but the whole time they're scamming you. It can make you so mad that you don't trust anybody.

It's infuriating even if you're a prizewinning manipulator like Jacob. He scammed his father and his brother, only to be out-scammed by his uncle Laban. God was teaching him, and he didn't like it one bit.

It's been said, "You can't run away from trouble. There's no place that far." Jacob ran from his angry brother, Esau, all the way back to the land where his grandfather Abraham was born. Now, after twenty years, he gets himself into a situation where he's running again, this time from Laban, and this time much more slowly because he has wives, children, servants, and flocks with him. The only place he can go is back to the land God promised to give Abraham. Back toward Esau.

fyi

Poplar . . . white (30:37). This is a pun. Laban's name means "white" in Hebrew, and it sounds like the Hebrew word for "poplar." Ancient people believed that if a pregnant animal had a vivid vision, it would leave a mark on the baby they were carrying. Jacob may have thought he was double-crossing Laban with magic, but in fact only God's generous intervention enabled Jacob to triumph over Laban.

1 Read Genesis 30:25-31:55. Make a list of who tries to deceive or cheat whom, and how, throughout this episode.

2 Has Jacob succeeded because he is a better cheater than Laban? What does Jacob say about this in 31:10-13? In 31:41-42?

3 Why do you think he calls God "the Fear of Isaac" in 31:42?

4   Read Genesis 32:1-32. Jacob is scared to face his brother (32:7). How does he deal with his fear?

32:7-8

32:9-12

32:13-21

5   What do his actions say about how he's changed and not changed?

6   Compare what he says to God in 32:9-12 with what he said in 28:20-22. How has his relationship with God grown?

fyi   *Name (32:27,29).* Ancient people believed that someone's name revealed his character, so it was an act of trust to tell your name. Knowing someone's name was thought to give you a psychological advantage over him. God gave Adam the right to name the animals (2:19-20), and God gave new names to Abram/Abraham, Sarai/Sarah, Isaac, and now Jacob/Israel.

7 In Genesis 32:22-32, who do you think is the man that Jacob wrestles with? What makes you think that?

8 How has Jacob struggled with God during his life?

Present (33:11). This is the same Hebrew word as "blessing" in 27:35. Jacob stole Esau's blessing, but now he wants to return one, a tiny part of the blessing God gave him freely.

9 Read Genesis 33:1-20. What, if anything, surprises you about Esau's actions in this episode? Or why are you not surprised?

live

10 In what ways do you wrestle with God or about God?

11 What would you like to say to God in response to Jacob's story?

connect

Talk about the ways you wrestle with God or about God. Then pray together for each person who is wrestling. Ask God to give each person the strength to refuse to let go of Him until He blesses you.

go deeper

Examine the effects of the Fall and human sin on these women from Genesis: Sarah (12:11-15; 16:1-6; 18:9-15; 20:1-2; 21:8-10); Hagar (16:1-16; 21:8-21); Rebekah (25:28; 26:7; 27:5-17,42-46); Rachel (30:1-24; 31:14-16,19; 35:16-18); Leah (29:16-30); Dinah (34:1-21). How do people treat each woman? How does each woman behave?

memory verse of the week

Did a particular verse make you think? Is there a verse you can't get out of your head? Write it down and memorize it. Allow God's Word to permanently brand itself in your head and your heart.

notes from group discussion

notes from group discussion

joseph and his brothers

Lesson 10

You intended to harm me, but God intended it for good to accomplish what is now being done, the saving of many lives.

Genesis 50:20

If you have brothers or sisters, you probably know that life in a family is not always one long love fest. It can seem like you have to fight every minute for your stuff, your space, your status. It's even worse when parents play favorites, and if your siblings are half-siblings or step-siblings in a blended family, things can get truly complicated – sometimes even ugly.

Jacob had twelve sons and a daughter by two full wives and two servant-wives. What a soap opera! Joseph was the next-to-youngest child, and his story is a great tale of suspense, humor, secret identities, and sudden reversals. But as fun as the story is, its main character is not Joseph but God, who engineers the whole thing in order to turn the rough-and-tumble family of Jacob into the nation of Israel.

1 Read straight through Genesis 37:1–50:26. It's a fun story. You can skip chapters 38 and 49 if you need to. As you read, answer the following questions:

What does *God allow to happen* in each episode?

What does *God do*?

What *character qualities* does Joseph show at each point in the story? How is he consistent? How does he grow over time?

What *character qualities* do other people show?

2 What are God's goals in allowing Joseph to go through so much suffering (45:4-11; 46:2-4)? See also 15:13-14.

3   God promised to bless the nations through Abraham's descendants (12:3). How has this begun to be fulfilled by the end of Genesis?

4   What do God's goals and actions in the lives of Jacob and his sons tell you about Him?

live

5   Did Joseph know God's reasons for what he was going through while he was going through it? How might this affect the way you deal with the things you're going through?

6   Talk with God about your situation. Do you wonder if He is with you the way He was with Joseph (39:2,3,21,23)? If you do, tell Him that. If you're confident of His presence, thank Him for that.

connect

Talk about where this study has taken you. What have you gotten out of it personally? Has the group itself meant anything to you that you're grateful for? Do you still have any unanswered questions that this study raised? How can this group help you as you continue to play your part in the story of God and His people?

This is a good time to pray for each person in the group, one at a time. Tell God something about this person that you're grateful for, and ask Him to work in this person to strengthen things like courage in hard circumstances, and trust that God is present and active for good.

go deeper

Just as Genesis includes the genealogies (family lines from father to son) of its key characters, so also the New Testament begins with a genealogy of Jesus. Read Matthew 1:1-3. Why do you think the New Testament begins like this? Notice in particular verse 3, and read the story of Tamar in Genesis 38. Why do you think Matthew makes a point of naming Tamar in Jesus' family line? What does the inclusion of her story in Jesus' story say about Jesus' human lineage? About His calling as the Savior? Do you think Tamar would have been surprised to have her name included with such honor? Why or why not?

memory verse of the week

Did a particular verse make you think? Is there a verse you can't get out of your head? Write it down and memorize it. Allow God's Word to permanently brand itself in your head and your heart.

notes from group discussion

study resources

Studying the Bible can lead you to answers to life's tough questions. But Bible study also prompts plenty of *new* questions. Perhaps you're intrigued by a passage and want to understand it better. Maybe you're stumped about what a particular verse or word means. Where do you go from here? Study resources can help. Research a verse's history, cultural context, and connotations. Look up unfamiliar words. Track down related Scripture passages elsewhere in the Bible. Study resources can help sharpen your knowledge of God's Word.

On the following pages you'll find a selected bibliography of study resources. Use them to discover more, dig deeper, and ultimately grow closer to God.

additional Bible translations

If you want to know what a particular phrase or passage means, your first and easiest resource is usually another reliable Bible translation. *Biblegateway.com* offers more than two dozen English translations, including many of those that are most popular today. You can type in the verse reference you're interested in and quickly see how half a dozen other versions translate it. The options range from highly literal word-for-word translations like the New American Standard Bible, to the freer thought-for-thought translations like the New International Version, to a robust and thought-provoking paraphrase like *The Message.*

concordances

If you're studying a specific word or phrase and want to know how it's used throughout a particular book, the New Testament, or the whole Bible, use a concordance. A concordance lists every verse in the Bible in which that word shows up. *Strong's Exhaustive Concordance* and

Young's Analytical Concordance of the Bible have been the standard printed concordances for decades. They will also let you know which Greek or Hebrew word is used in each case.

If you prefer to search online, *Biblegateway.com* allows you to quickly search any of its Bible versions, or multiple ones, for a word or phrase. *E-sword.net* software enables you to search for a specific Greek or Hebrew word.

dictionaries

A good English dictionary is often useful if, for example, you don't know what "threshing" means. *Merriam-Webster.com* is a good dictionary available free online.

A Bible dictionary or Bible encyclopedia alphabetically lists articles about people, places, doctrines, important words, customs, and geography of the Bible. *Blueletterbible.org* offers an older version of the *International Standard Bible Encyclopaedia* free online. Here are a few up-to-date dictionaries to consider:

Mounce's Complete Expository Dictionary of Old and New Testament Words. Grand Rapids, MI: Zondervan, 2006.
Accurate, in-depth definitions reflecting current scholarship. Keyed to several translations. Each English entry discusses both Old Testament (Hebrew) and New Testament (Greek) words when applicable.

The New Unger's Bible Dictionary, Revised and Expanded. Wheaton, IL: Moody, 2006.
More than 6,700 entries reflecting current scholarship and more than 1,200,000 words. Includes detailed essays, photographs, maps, charts, and illustrations. Based on the New American Standard Version, but cross-referenced to most major Bible translations.

Vine's Complete Expository Dictionary of Old and New Testament Words. Nashville: Nelson, 1996.

Combines Vine's Expository Dictionary of New Testament Words *and* Unger and White's *Expository Dictionary of the Old Testament.* Lets you look up English equivalents of the Greek or Hebrew words from which they are translated. Illustrates significant words with Scripture passages, comments, crossreferences, ancient and modern meanings, etymologies, and historical notes. Not as current as the two references listed on the previous page, but popular and easy to use.*

historical and background sources

D. A. Carson and Douglas J. Moo. *An Introduction to the New Testament,* 2nd Edition. Grand Rapids, MI: Zondervan, 2005.

Addresses authorship, date, sources, purpose, destination, literary form, and more about each biblical book, as well as a summary of the book's content and its theological contribution to the Bible. A reliable evangelical treatment of the issues.

J. Daniel Hays and J. Scott Duvall. *The Baker Illustrated Bible Handbook.* Grand Rapids, MI: Baker, 2011.

Treats each biblical book in detail and places it within the Grand Story of the Bible. The history surrounding each book is explained in accessible language, then the message of each book is applied directly to our lives.

Craig S. Keener. *The IVP Bible Background Commentary: New Testament.* Downers Grove, IL: InterVarsity, 1993.

In verse-by-verse format this one-volume commentary gives the crucial cultural background needed for rich Bible study. Includes a glossary of cultural terms and historical figures, maps, and charts, as well as introductory essays with cultural background information for each New Testament book.

Mark Allan Powell. *Introducing the New Testament: A Historical, Literary, and Theological Survey.* Grand Rapids, MI: Baker, 2009.

Treats controversial issues without favoring traditional or skeptical perspectives, so it leaves space for the student or the church to come to conclusions. Includes works of Christian art related to biblical passages from the first to twenty-first centuries. Lots of material on the associated website.

Christopher R. Smith. *Read the Bible Smarter, Not Harder: Exploring the Stories Behind the Books.* Colorado Springs, CO: Biblica, 2011.

Helps readers get the point of whole books of the Bible rather than focusing on individual verses or chapters. Introduces each book of the Bible, explaining why it was written, what kind of writing it is, how it's put together, and what major themes and ideas it develops.

Bible atlases

We often skim over mentions of specific locations in the Bible, but location is an important element to understanding the context of a passage. A Bible atlas can help you understand the geography in a book of the Bible and how it may have affected recorded events. Online searches can provide a lot of useful information, but because the Internet isn't always accurate, here are two good atlases to consider:

John D. Currid and David P. Barrett. *Crossway ESV Bible Atlas.* Wheaton, IL: Crossway, 2010.

Historical, modern, and scientific maps produced by satellite technology. Excellent written content on the geography of biblical places. Available in either print or e-book.

Carl G. Rasmussen. *Zondervan Atlas of the Bible*. Grand Rapids, MI: Zondervan, 2009.

Updated with the latest scholarship, 3-D imaging, and excellent photos. Expanded introduction; maps of Greece, Turkey, and Italy; a historical progression through the Old and New Testaments; and chapters on biblical archaeology, geography, and the history of Jerusalem.

for small-group leaders

If you lead a small group or would like to lead one, these resources may help:

Bill Donahue. *Leading Life-Changing Small Groups, Revised*. Grand Rapids, MI: Zondervan, 2002.

Sets out a philosophy of what small groups are for, explains how to use them for discipleship, and teaches how to conduct meetings. Contains updated charts, diagrams, and resource lists.

Neal F. McBride. *How to Lead Small Groups*. Colorado Springs, CO: NavPress, 1990.

Covers leadership skills and gives step-by-step guidance and practical exercises for the most important aspects of group leadership.

Laurie Polich. *Help! I'm a Small-Group Leader*. Grand Rapids, MI: Zondervan/Youth Specialties, 1998.

Offers tips and solutions to help you nurture your small group and accomplish your goals. Suggests techniques and questions to use in many Bible study circumstances. Geared especially to high school groups.

Bible study methods

Gordon Fee and Douglas Stuart. *How to Read the Bible for All Its Worth*. Grand Rapids, MI: Zondervan, 2005.

Offers chapters on interpreting and applying the different kinds of writing in the Bible: Epistles, Gospels, Old Testament Law, Old Testament narrative, the Prophets, Psalms, Wisdom, and Revelation. Also suggests comments on each book of the Bible.

Jen Hatmaker. *A Modern Girl's Guide to Bible Study*. Colorado Springs, CO: NavPress, 2006.

A fun and entertaining guide to serious Bible study designed for young women.

Oletta Wald. *The New Joy of Discovery in Bible Study*. Minneapolis, MN: Augsburg, 2002.

Helps students of Scripture discover how to observe all that is in a text, how to ask questions of a text, and how to use grammar and passage structure to see the writer's point. Teaches methods of independent Bible study.

MY LIFE IS **TOUGHER** THAN MOST **PEOPLE REALIZE.**

I TRY TO KEEP EVERYTHING IN BALANCE: FRIENDS, FAMILY, WORK, SCHOOL, AND GOD.

IT'S NOT EASY.

I KNOW WHAT MY PARENTS BELIEVE AND WHAT MY PASTOR SAYS.

BUT IT'S NOT ABOUT THEM. IT'S ABOUT ME...

ISN'T IT TIME I OWN MY FAITH?

THROUGH THICK AND THIN, KEEP YOUR HEARTS AT ATTENTION, IN ADORATION BEFORE CHRIST, YOUR MASTER. BE READY TO SPEAK UP AND TELL ANYONE WHO ASKS WHY YOU'RE LIVING THE WAY YOU ARE, AND ALWAYS WITH THE UTMOST COURTESY. 1 PETER 3:15 (MSG)

www.navpress.com | 1-800-366-7788

THINK **TH1NK** *by* **NAVPRESS**

SUPPORT THE MINISTRY OF THE NAVIGATORS

The Navigators' calling is to advance the gospel of Jesus and His kingdom into the nations through spiritual generations of laborers living and discipling among the lost.

Navigators have invested their lives in people for more than 75 years, coming alongside them life on life to help them passionately know Christ and to make Him known.

The U.S. Navigators' ministry touches lives in varied settings, including college campuses, military bases, downtown offices, urban neighborhoods, prisons, and youth camps.

Dedicated to helping people navigate spiritually, The Navigators aims to make a permanent difference in the lives of people around the world. The Navigators helps its communities of friends to follow Christ passionately and equip them effectively to go out and do the same.

To learn more about donating to The Navigators' ministry,
go to **www.navigators.org/us/support**
or call toll-free at **1-866-568-7827**.